# STUMPED!

## The world's funniest cricket quotes

By Charlie Croker

Crombie Jardine
Publishing Limited
Office 2
3 Edgar Buildings
George Street
Bath
BA1 2FJ
www.crombiejardine.com

ISBN 978-1-906051-02-0

First published by Crombie Jardine Publishing Limited, 2008

Printed and bound in China

# Contents

# Introduction

A great deal of credit must go to cricket radio announcers. Whilst most sports commentators have at best a couple of hours to fill, our cricket announcers have up to eight hours to spend keeping us informed and entertained. It is no wonder that they come out with the occasional howler or downright gaffe. The master of these was, of course, Brian Johnston.

Born in 1912 in Little Berkhamsted, Hertfordshire, Johnston was educated at Eton and New College, Oxford. He joined the BBC in January 1946, after service with the Grenadier Guards in the Second World War in which he won the Military Cross. He began his cricket commentating career at Lord's for BBC Television in June 1946 at the England v India Test match. On 22 April 1948 he married Pauline Tozer. They had five children.

From 1965 onwards, Johnston split his commentary duties between television (three Tests) and radio (two Tests) each summer. In 1970 Johnston was dropped from the TV commentary team but continued to appear as a member of the Test Match Special (TMS) radio team. He retired from the BBC in 1972 on his sixtieth birthday and became a freelance commentator and it was in that capacity that he continued to appear on TMS for the next twenty-two years.

In one famous incident during a Test match at the Oval, Jonathan Agnew suggested that Ian Botham was out because he had failed to "get his leg over". Johnston carried on commentating (and giggling) for thirty seconds before finally dissolving into helpless laughter. All over Britain drivers listening to Test Match Special were forced to pull over as this incident made it impossible to drive safely.

Another of Johnston's gaffes came about when Neil Harvey was representing Australia at the Headingley Test in 1961: "There's Neil Harvey standing at leg slip with his legs wide apart, waiting for a tickle." The oft-cited quote — "The bowler's Holding, the batsman's Willey" — allegedly occurred when Michael Holding of the West Indies was bowling to Peter Willey of England in a Test match at the Oval in 1976. Johnston apparently claimed not to have noticed saying anything odd during the match, and that he was only alerted to his gaffe by a letter from "a lady" named "Miss Mainpiece". According to Christopher Martin-Jenkins, and the biography of Brian by Johnston's son Barry, Johnston never actually made the remark. His son says, "It was too good a pun to resist... but Brian never actually said that he had spoken the words on air." However, this is contradicted by an account offered by Henry Blofeld, who was present at the time. It really does not matter if he said it or not as it has gone down, good-naturedly, in the folklore of cricket.

This book is dedicated to cricket people the world over. It's a sport that doesn't take itself too seriously and it's all the better for that.

If we have missed out your favourite quote or gaffe, please send it to us at admin@crombiejardine.com; it may make the next edition. Many thanks.

# *Stumped!*

"A very small crowd here today. I can count the
people on one hand. Can't be more than 30"
*Michael Abrahamson*

"The breeze is getting up and we can just
about see Umpire Shepherd's trousers
filling up with wind"
*Jonathan Agnew*

"He scored one or two boundaries in his seven"
*Jonathan Agnew*

"It's hit high in the air, it's safe and... out!"
*Jonathan Agnew*

# The world's funniest cricket quotes

"The Zimbabwean fans have been quite quiet;
now there are dozens of them starting to expose
themselves"
*Jonathan Agnew*

"It's a beautiful day today and as I look around
the ground I can see about 30 young girls all
wearing Dutch caps"
*Jonathan Agnew*

"Andy Caddick's shadow is longer than he is, and
he's a very tall man"
*Jonathan Agnew*

"Gel is more macho than a hairband"
*Wasim Akram on the benefits of hair gel
in the 1990s*

"Umpire Fenwick just itches his nose, rather than putting his finger up in the usual fashion"
*Paul Allott*

"On the outfield, hundreds of small boys are playing with their balls"
*Rex Alston*

"It's a very psychological sport, cricket — once the kingpin goes down, all the other puzzles just crumble away"
*Anita Anand*

"I feel I have had a very interesting life, but I am rather hoping there is still more to come. I still haven't captained the England cricket team, or sung at Carnegie Hall!"
*Jeffrey Archer*

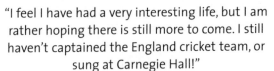

"... and Ray Illingworth is relieving himself in
front of the pavilion"
*John Arlott*

"Bill Frindall has done a bit of mental arithmetic
with a calculator"
*John Arlott*

"I presented my trousers to the committee: I had
nothing to hide"
*Mike Atherton*

"This morning he [Marcus Trescothick] has more
or less left off where he carried on yesterday
afternoon"
*Mike Atherton*

"When you restrict a side to 170, 99 times out of
ten you feel confident"
*Mike Atherton*

"To win a three match series you really want to
be looking at winning two of the matches"
*Mike Atherton*

### Trevor Edward Bailey (b.1923)

Bailey was a talented English Test cricketer. A right-arm fast bowler, dependable and often dour right-handed batsman and brilliant fielder, Bailey played 61 Tests for England between 1949 and 1959. He took 132 wickets at the bowling average of 29, scored a century (134 not out) in attaining a very useful batting average of nearly 30, and took 32 catches. Perhaps his most famous achievement came at the Lord's Test in 1953 when, with England apparently facing defeat, he shared a defensive fifth wicket stand with Willie Watson, defying the Australian bowlers for over four hours to earn a draw. England went on to regain The Ashes.

In 1967, Bailey became a cricket journalist and broadcaster. He was a regular on the BBC's Test Match Special for many years, where fellow commentator Brian Johnston nicknamed him "The Boil", based on the Australian barrackers' supposed pronunciation of his name as "Boiley".

"The obvious successor to Brearley at the
moment isn't obvious"
*Trevor Bailey*

"There are good one-day players, there are
good Test players, and vice-versa"
*Trevor Bailey*

"He's on 90... ten away from that
mythical figure"
*Trevor Bailey*

"It's especially tense for Parker who's
literally fighting for a place on an
overcrowded plane to India"
*Trevor Bailey*

"Sean Pollock there, a carbon copy of his dad.
Except he's a bit taller and he's got red hair"
*Trevor Bailey*

"Tavare has literally dropped anchor"
*Trevor Bailey*

"His tail is literally up"
*Trevor Bailey*

"A wicket could always fall in this game,
literally at any time"
*Trevor Bailey*

"No captain with all the hindsight in the world
can predict how the wicket is going to play"
*Trevor Bailey*

"The first time you face up to a googly you're
going to be in trouble if you've never faced one
before"
*Trevor Bailey*

"I don't think he expected it, and that's what
caught him unawares"
*Trevor Bailey*

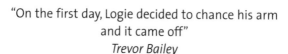

"On the first day, Logie decided to chance his arm
and it came off"
*Trevor Bailey*

"We owe some gratitude to Gatting and Lamb,
who breathed some life into a corpse which had
nearly expired"
*Trevor Bailey*

"Then there was that dark horse with the golden
arm, Mudassar Nazar'
*Trevor Bailey*

"This series has been swings and pendulums all
the way through"
*Trevor Bailey*

"The Port Elizabeth ground is more of a circle
than an oval. It's long and square"
*Trevor Bailey*

"The batting side find it easier to bat in bad light
than the fielding side do"
*Trevor Bailey*

"An aggressive back foot drive off the back foot..."
*Trevor Bailey*

"Nigeria — very much the dark horses of
this tournament"
*Rob Bailey*

"Malcolm Marshall scored a handful of runs at
Headingley... nought and one"
*Jack Bannister*

"Mudassar has really put the icing on the day
for the visitors"
*Jack Bannister*

"That's another nail in what looks like being
a very good score"
*Jack Bannister*

"And the rest not only is history, but will remain
history for many years to come"
*Jack Bannister*

"Well, Wally, I've been watching this game, both
visually and on TV"
*Ken Barrington*

"Now Ramprakash is facing a fish of a rather
different feather in Mark Waugh"
*Peter Baxter*

"Zimbabwe have done well, just as it looked as
though the horse had left the stable and gone
galloping down the road, they managed to put a
chain on the door"
*Peter Baxter*

"And now an erect MCC member has been sat
down... and this slightly sticky period continues"
*BBC commentator*

"He [Courtney Walsh] ripped the heart out of
England, both metaphorically and physically"
*BBC commentator*

### Richard "Richie" Benaud OBE (b.1930)

A former Australian cricketer, and one of the greatest leg-spinners to have played Test cricket, Benaud has become one of the most recognisable and popular commentators in the game.

After retiring from playing in 1963, Benaud turned to full-time cricket journalism and commentary, dividing his time between Britain (where he worked for the BBC for many years, prior to joining Channel 4) and Australia (for Nine Network). Overall he played in or commentated on approximately 500 Test matches.

With Channel 4's loss of the rights to broadcast live Test match cricket to Sky Sports, the 2005 Ashes series was the last that Benaud commentated on in Britain.

~

"Yorkshire all out 232, Hutton ill!
I'm sorry. Hutton 111"
*BBC news announcer*

"Whenever they win the toss, for example, South
Africa either bat first or field first"
*Tony Becca*

"It was a bit strange walking out to the middle
with no players out there"
*Ian Bell*

"Captaincy is 90% luck and 10% skill"
*Richie Benaud*

"The replay, which the umpire doesn't have the benefit of, shows that he was either an inch in or an inch out"
*Richie Benaud*

"... nearly 34 — in fact he's 33"
*Richie Benaud*

"A church spire nestling among the trees... there's probably a church there too"
*Richie Benaud*

"That slow motion replay doesn't show how fast the ball was travelling"
*Richie Benaud*

"This shirt is unique, there are only 200 of them"
*Richie Benaud*

"Even Downton couldn't get down high
enough for that"
*Richie Benaud*

"The only possible result is a draw. The alternative
is a win for England"
*Richie Benaud*

"The spectators are jumping around like dervishes
at a teddy bears' picnic"
*Richie Benaud*

"Because out in the field, you haven't got anyone whispering into your ear saying all sorts of things, you've got to do it yourself"
*Richie Benaud*

"There were no scores below single figures"
*Richie Benaud*

"His throw went absolutely nowhere near where it was going"
*Richie Benaud*

"There are a lot of hookers around the world"
*Richie Benaud*

"The hallmark of a great captain is his ability to
win the toss at the right time"
*Richie Benaud*

"And for Fidel Castro, there's an extra man placed
on the midwicket boundary"
*Richie Benaud referring to Fidel Edwards*

"Laird has been brought in to stand in
the corner of the circle"
*Richie Benaud*

"There were congratulations and high sixes
all round"
*Richie Benaud*

"He's usually a good puller — but he couldn't get it up that time"
*Richie Benaud*

"And it's time for a glass of something chilled"
*Richie Benaud*

"Taking It From Behind"
*Title of wicketkeeper Richard Blakey's autobiography*

"It's been a very slow and dull day, but it hasn't been boring. It's been a good, entertaining day's cricket"
*Tony Benneworth*

### Henry Calthorpe Blofeld (b.1939)

Known as "Blowers", thanks to the late Brian Johnston, Blofeld is possibly best known for his cricket commentory for BBC Radio 4, although he also commentated for ITV in the 1960s and for BSkyB from 1991 to 1994.

His cricket commentary is famous and admired for his rich and mellow voice and his particular mention of superfluous detail, such as pigeons, buses, and helicopters that happen to be passing by. He frequently makes mistakes (often not being able to identify players) and is quite often lost for words in the more exciting passages of play but this doesn't seem to matter one jot to the many loyal listeners to TMS over the world. Indeed, his popularity was highlighted in a Test against Pakistan at Headingley in 1996, when a flat overlooking the ground was draped with a huge banner proclaiming "Henry Blofeld is God".

"Their heads were on their chins"
*Henry Blofeld*

# Stumped!

"Klusener holds that bat like a piece of wood"
*Henry Blofeld*

"He's laid out his stall and is sticking to it"
*Henry Blofeld*

"Radio 4 listeners, you are back after the most exciting shipping forecast there's ever been, except you didn't hear it because it was happening here at Lord's"
*Henry Blofeld*

"It's a catch he would have caught 99 times out of 1000"
*Henry Blofeld*

"It's awfully uncomfortable to have McGrath
up your sleeve, isn't it?"
*Henry Blofeld*

"We might be in for more rain than
maybe we're going to get"
*Henry Blofeld*

"He's standing on one leg like a horse in a
dressage competition"
*Henry Blofeld*

"The lights are shining quite darkly"
*Henry Blofeld*

"It is a full house at the Eden Gardens. Today,
Calcutta is celebrating the assassination of
Mahatma Gandhi"
*Henry Blofeld*

"He's eternally left-handed"
*Henry Blofeld about Ashley Giles*

"He [Trescothick] threw at that:
the kitchen sink, the bath and everything else
in that room as well"
*Henry Blofeld*

"I hope no one's house is burning down. It's much
too nice a day to be left without a house"
*Henry Blofeld*

"In the rear, the small diminutive figure of Shoaib
Mohammed, who can't be much taller or shorter
than he is"
*Henry Blofeld*

"Oh, and here comes Caddick to bowl again from
the pavilion end again — well, I don't suppose
he'll mind if I read the scores between his balls"
*Henry Blofeld*

"He came in from the outfield there like an
absolute rabbit"
*Henry Blofeld*

"In Hampshire's innings the Smith brothers
scored 13 and 52 respectively"
*Henry Blofeld*

"His absence can never quite be replaced
here at Lord's"
*Henry Blofeld*

"He is like a guardsman. Every part of him erect"
*Henry Blofeld*

"If the tension here was a block of cheddar
cheese you could cut it with a knife"
*Henry Blofeld*

"England need to pick players who do not have
skeletons in their coffins"
*Ian Botham*

"He [Courtney Walsh] has had a rest, Mikey, and a
rest is as good as a break"
*Ian Botham*

"At the end of the day it's September"
*Ian Botham*

"I am colour-blind, which makes me worry
about what clothes I put on in the morning. My
wife matches my shirts and ties in advance"
*Ian Botham*

"Pakistan is the sort of place every man
should send his mother-in-law, for a month,
with all expenses paid"
*Ian Botham*

### Geoffrey Boycott (b.1940)

A former Yorkshire and England cricketer, Boycott had a successful career from 1962 to 1986, establishing himself as one of England's finest opening batsmen. His highest Test score was 246 not out in June 1967, but he was dropped from the next match for slow scoring. He spent from 1974 to 1977 in self-imposed exile from the England team, claiming he had simply lost his appetite for Test cricket.

Later, Boycott became an often outspoken cricket commentator for both radio and television, adopting a 'tell-it-how-it-is' style delivery, and is consequently known for criticizing players. On one particular occasion, after witnessing a dropped catch, he remarked, "I reckon my mum could have caught that in her pinny."

Here are some classic Boycottisms...

～

"To stay in, you've got to not get out"
*Geoff Boycott*

"It would be unprintable on television"
*Geoff Boycott*

"If England lose now, they will be leaving the
field with their heads between their legs"
*Geoff Boycott*

"I'm glad two sides of the cherry
have been put forward"
*Geoff Boycott*

"I would die tomorrow if I could have five more years to play cricket for Yorkshire and England"
*Geoff Boycott*

"The only way they'll get a wicket is if the ball hits a brick in the middle of the pitch... it wouldn't frighten me mum, this bowling"
*Geoff Boycott*

"We don't want umpires to be allowed to play God like this ever again"
*Geoff Boycott on Darrell Hair*

"All these ICC officials sitting in their tax haven in Dubai and saying 'the umpire's always right' — that's not going to help anyone. They've got to forget about their big egos for a moment and let us move on"
*Geoff Boycott*

"I'll cross that chestnut when we get to it"
*Geoff Boycott*

"Glenn McGrath bowled so badly in
his first Test, as though he'd never bowled
in a Test match before"
*Geoff Boycott*

"Such an easy pitch... Graham Gooch and Alec
Stewart think their Christmases have all come home"
*Geoff Boycott*

"He's bowling fast, which is what you want from
a pace bowler"
*Geoff Boycott*

"This idea that umpires are always right is a load of old cobblers. What I want to know is: Who umpires the umpires? The players suffer from their mistakes, but no one ever seems to get rid of the umpires themselves. Being an umpire is a people job: that's why Dickie Bird was good at it. Yes, he was a loony, and he made mistakes — everyone does. But he knew how to deal with people, so they respected him"
*Geoff Boycott*

"It is physically and mentally soul-destroying"
*Geoff Boycott*

"Defreitas — just in the back of his mind he is wearing a support"
*Geoff Boycott*

"You've got to make split-second decisions
so quickly"
*Geoff Boycott*
❦

"Fortunately it was a slow ball —
so it wasn't a fast one"
*Geoff Boycott*
❦

"As the ball gets softer it loses its hardness"
*Geoff Boycott*
❦

"[Gavin Larsen] is inexperienced in Test cricket, in
that this is his first Test"
*Geoff Boycott*
❦

"... and England win by a solitary nine runs..."
*Frank Bough*

"After their 60 overs, West Indies have scored 244
for 7, all out"
*Frank Bough*

"Playing against a team with Ian Chappell as
captain turns a cricket match into gang warfare"
*Mike Brearley*

"Alderman knows that he's either going
to get a wicket, or he isn't"
*Steve Brenkley*

"You almost run out of expletives
for this man's fielding"
*Chris Broad*

"He is big and brash and as subtle
as colonic irrigation"
*Rick Broadbent on Kevin Pietersen*

"It's got nothing to do with cricket — it's all
about how good you look on the beach"
*Mark Butcher*

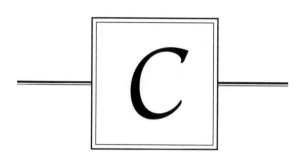

"My cricket's all been played in a triangle of
about two or three square miles"
*Phil Carrick*

"It's tough for a natural hooker to give it up"
*Ian Chappell*

"Shake It Up Baby"
*Title of song being played at a cricket match,
according to Ian Chappell. It was actually "Twist
and Shout"*

"Fast bowlers are quick, even at the end
of the day. Just watch this — admittedly
it's in slow motion"
*Ian Chappell*

"The other advantage England have got when
Phil Tufnell is bowling is that he is not fielding"
*Ian Chappell*

"Now this next question has absolutely nothing
to do with either music or sport: at what ground
did Geoff Boycott hit his hundredth hundred?"
*Classic FM*

"The Test Match begins in ten minutes — that's
our time, of course..."
*David Coleman*

"As a result, Tasmania picks up two valuable
points, not that they are any value now. The
match has already been decided"
*Gerry Collins*

"Matthew Hoggard has been living in an oxygen
chamber since injuring his hand, so his mobile
signal has been off and I haven't been able to
catch up with him yet"
*Paul Collingwood*

"That was a sort of parson's nose innings —
good in parts"
*Charles Colville*

"Sri Lanka 1 for 68. The scoreboard shows 1 for 67.
That correct? It is? Thanks, Jack. Another single.
One for 66"
*Dennis Cometti*

"Trying to get a ball past him is like trying to
sneak a sunrise past a rooster"
*Jeremy Coney on bowling to Brian Lara*

"I'll take an ugly 100 over a pretty 10 any day"
*Alastair Cook*

"It's half of one, six-a-dozen of the other"
*Chris Cowdrey*

"Skipper Moin Khan has really earned his socks
out there today"
*Chris Cowdrey*

"England have their noses in front — not only
actually, but metaphorically too"
*Tony Cozier*

"The Queen's Park Oval, exactly as its name
suggests — absolutely round"
*Tony Cozier*

"Now Botham, with a chance to put everything
that has gone before behind him"
*Tony Cozier*

"Mike Atherton's a thinking captain.
He gives the impression of someone with his
head on all the time"
*Colin Croft*

# Stumped!

"The only person who could be better than Brian
Lara could be Brian Lara himself"
*Colin Croft*

"Pakistan always have the same problem — too
many chiefs and not enough Indians"
*Robert Croft*

*In 1999, as Daryll Cullinan was on his way to
the wicket, a mischievous Shane Warne
commented that he'd been waiting two years
for another chance to humiliate Cullinan.
The latter apparently responded quick as a flash
with a humorous:*
*"Looks like you've spent it eating"*

"Even my father can play club cricket in England"
*Zimbabwe coach Kevin Curran*

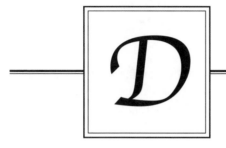

"England were beaten in the sense
that they lost"
*Dickie Davis*

"David Boon is now completely clean-shaven,
except for his moustache"
*Graham Dawson*

"So that's 57 runs needed by Hampshire in 11
overs, and it doesn't need a calculator to tell you
that the run rate required is 5.1818"
*Norman DeMesquita*

"He's no mean slouch as a bowler"
*Mike Denness*

"That's a remarkable catch by Yardley, especially as the ball quite literally rolled along the ground towards him"
*Mike Denness*

"If you're going to lose, you might as well lose good and proper and try to sneak a win"
*Ted Dexter*

"The last rites are on the wall here"
*Allan Donald*

"I'm not bothered about ratings or rankings from ICC. I don't even look at that"
*Rahul Dravid delivering the good news to the ICC*

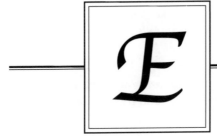

"This game was another rung on the ladder of
the learning curve"
*John Emburey*

"Pakistan can play well, but they have the ability
to play badly too"
*John Emburey*

"There must be something on Gooch's mind and
he wants to get it off his chest"
*Farokh Engineer*

"If Gower had stopped that he would have
decapitated his hand"
*Farokh Engineer*

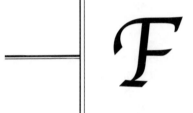

"I have found a new method to avoid bowling no-balls by measuring my leap before delivery and my run up. I don't think I will in future bowl no-balls"
*Dilhara Fernando*

"They're very experienced Test players with a lot of caps under them"
*Duncan Fletcher*

"Matthew Hoggard called the Prime Minister a knob when we were celebrating winning the Ashes at a Downing Street function, and you know what? That's the first thing Hoggy's got right in a while. Blair *is* a knob"
*England captain Andrew Flintoff*

# G

# *The world's funniest cricket quotes*

"The wicket didn't do too much, but when it did, it did too much"
*Mike Gatting*

"I hurt my thumb and then obviously the mother-in-law died"
*Mike Gatting*

"Question: Do you feel that the selectors and yourself have been vindicated by the result?
Answer: I don't think the press are vindictive. They can write what they want"
*Mike Gatting*

"[I am] not a good watcher of the game... I think cricket is a boring game to watch"
*Sunil Gavaskar*

"Srikkanth is a vegetarian. If he swallows a fly he
will be in trouble"
*Sunil Gavaskar*

"A couple of the Indian fielders now are
streaming out very slowly"
*Sunil Gavaskar*

"Glenn McGrath joins Craig McDermott and
Paul Reiffel in a three-ponged prace attack"
*Tim Gavel*

"I've had the hip problem and the hip
problem is still there. Which came first —
the groin or the hip?"
*Ashley Giles*

"You have to clap yourself on at the WACA"
*NSW all-rounder Gary Gilmour*

"If we can beat South Africa on Saturday that
will be a great fillip in our cap"
*Graham Gooch*

"The Sri Lankan team have lost their
heads, literally"
*Gamine Goonasena*

"When I first started playing we went to the pub
to talk cricket and we used to learn that way,
over three or four or five pints. Now you very
rarely see that. I'm old-school so I do miss that"
*Darren Gough*

# Stumped!

"At school it should be compulsory
to learn the waltz"
*Darren Gough*

"When you win the toss — bat. If you are in
doubt, think about it, then bat. If you have very
big doubts, consult a colleague — then bat"
*W. G. Grace*

"Yes, he's a very good cricketer — pity he's not a
better batter or bowler"
*Tom Graveney*

"In many ways this is Allan Lamb"
*Tom Graveney*

"The pattern of the match is certainly swaying
towards Kent"
*Tom Graveney*

"Once again our consistency has been proved to
be inconsistent"
*Tom Graveney*

"I think if you've got a safe pair of hands, you've
got a safe pair of hands"
*Tom Graveney*

"Is cricket in danger of becoming
a political football?"
*Kevin Greening*

### Anthony "Tony" William Greig (b.1946)

Although born in South Africa, Greig qualified to play for England by virtue of his Scottish father and became captain of the national side from 1975 to 1977.

Sometimes a controversial figure, Greig helped Kerry Packer start World Series Cricket by not only signing up many of his English colleagues but also West Indian and Pakistani cricketers; a daring act that cost him the captaincy of England. Packer later offered Greig a "job for life" as a commentator during Nine's cricket coverage.

Today, Greig lives in Australia and continues his commentary role. He has been criticized for his bias against the Australian team and for his occasional out-of-context comments. Greig also has commentated for Channel 4 in the UK.

≈

"In the back of Hughes' mind must be the thought that he will dance down the piss and mitch one"
*Tony Greig*
❅

"Lloyd's talking to his slippers"
*Tony Greig*
❅

"And Jajeda is dijappointed... Jadeja is ji..da.. I'll come again, Jajeda... okay... Jadeja looks downcast"
*Tony Greig*
❅

"What a magnificent shot! No, he's out"
*Tony Greig*
❅

"Clearly the West Indies are going to play their
normal game, which is what they normally do"
*Tony Greig*

"For every winner, there has to be a loser
in these games"
*Tony Greig*

"Marshall's bowling with his head"
*Tony Greig*

"Now, Pakistan are in real trouble"
*Tony Greig with Pakistan on 9/58*

"This run of 24 games without defeat — must
be like a millstone on your shoulders"
*Tony Gubba*

As in life so in death lies a bat of renown,
Slain by a lorry (three ton)
His innings is over, his bat is laid down;
To the end a poor judge of a run
*gravestone in England*

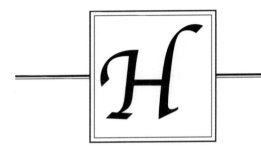

"One of the hardest things is to take a caught
and bowled off your own bowling"
*Mike Haysam*

"Everything in Halifax's favour is
against them tonight"
*Eddie Hemmings*

"I thought he was going to dive and decapitate
himself — badly"
*Mike Hendrick*

"These five weeks have passed at the
drop of a pin"
*Rachel Heyhoe-Flint*

"Cricket needs brightening up a bit.
My solution is to let players drink at the
beginning of the game, not after. It always
works in our picnic matches"
*Paul Hogan*

"Any team on their day can win the
World Cup. It takes two people to win
a game of one-day cricket. In five-day cricket,
it's team against team and it takes a lot more
than two people to win it"
*Matthew Hoggard*

"The hat trick started with the first wicket"
*Matthew Hoggard*

"You can ask any fast bowler. If he says he has never tampered with the ball, he either has just started playing, or is lying"
*Michael Holding*

"The most important thing about batting is getting the bat to hit the ball"
*Michael Holding*

"Cricket corruption is a rolling stone — it's gathering moss all the time"
*Oliver Holt*

"I don't know if this is his highest score in the John Player League. If not, this is his highest score"
*Robert Hudson*

"Look at Siddons. He's ready to throw
like a panther"
*Kim Hughes*

"When Merv leaves school, he is going to have to
be very good at football and cricket"
*Merv Hughes' fifth form geography report*

"Other than his mistakes, he hasn't put a foot
wrong"
*Simon Hughes*

"That black cloud is coming from the direction
the wind is blowing, now the wind is coming
from where the black cloud is"
*Ray Illingworth*

"He didn't drop the bat. It fell out of his hand"
*Ray Illingworth*

"I won't say it's easier, but it's easier"
*Ray Illingworth*

"He stood on tiptoe, on the back foot, and drove
the ball on the off. I don't know how you'd
describe that shot"
*Ray Illingworth*

"I don't want players who need a shoulder
to cry on"
*Ray Illingworth*

"There's no 'I' in team but there's
an 'I' in winners"
*Ronnie Irani*

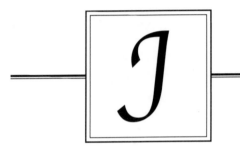

"Fourteen overs left, that's seven from each end"
*Robin Jackman*

"I can't bowl real well, I can't bat and I can't field... It's a big class rise but fingers crossed, I don't get a bat and just get a bit of a field"
*Andrew Johns coming clean about his skills*

"The open-topped bus ride around Trafalgar Square was a joyous moment in history, but if these things are graded by magnitude of achievement, England's reward for beating Sri Lanka will be a gentle spin in a milk float down Marylebone Road"
*Martin Johnson*

### Brian Alexander Johnston (1912-1994)

Known fondly as "Johnners", Johnston was a cricket commentator for the BBC from 1946 until his death. He began his cricket commentating career at Lord's for BBC Television in June 1946 at the England v India Test match.

Johnston was responsible for a number of the BBC's Test Match Special team's traditions, including giving nicknames to fellow commentators — Jonathan Agnew is still known as "Aggers", Henry Blofeld as "Blowers" and Bill Frindall as "the Bearded Wonder"!

Johnston's informal and humorous style was very popular. When he died, the *Daily Telegraph* described him as "the greatest natural broadcaster of them all", and John Major remarked that "summers will never be the same".

Johnston's memorial service was held at a crowded Westminster Abbey in May, 1994. The following year the Brian Johnston Memorial Trust was established, to promote cricket in schools and youth clubs, and to help young cricketers in need of financial support.

"Welcome to Worcester where you've just
missed seeing Barry Richards hitting one of Basil
D'Oliveira's balls clean out of the ground"
*Brian Johnston*

"There is a dirty black crowd here"
*Brian Johnston referring to a rain cloud over an
India-England match*

"Henry Horton's got a funny stance. It looks as if
he's shitting on a shooting stick"
*Brian Johnston*

"Massif Arsood"
*Brian Johnston trying to refer to Asif Masood*

"And a sedentary seagull flies by"
*Brian Johnston*

"Yes, I can see the happy couple now making
their way down the steps of the pavilion"
*Brian Johnston outside St Paul's Cathedral,
commentating on the wedding of Prince Charles
and Lady Diana Spencer*

"I don't think I have ever seen anything
quite like that before — it's the second time it's
happened today"
*Brian Johnston*

"Well, I shall remember that catch for many a
dying day"
*Brian Johnston*

"And I can see a strong wind blowing the sun
towards us"
*Brian Johnston*

"... and Dickie Bird standing there, with his neck
between his shoulders..."
*Brian Johnston*

"Ah yes, sledging. In the days before the
microphones on the pitch, we got that blind M.P.
chap up into the commentary box to lip-read"
*Brian Johnston*

"Top scorer so far is Watkinson with his 50 or
Atherton with his 40"
*Brian Johnston*

# Stumped!

"One ball left"
*Brian Johnston as Glenn Turner resumed batting*
*after being hit in an intimate place*

"He used to work for a very well-known firm —
can't remember who they are"
*Brian Johnston*

"Butcher plays this off the black foot"
*Brian Johnston*

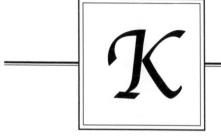

"Greg Chappell instructed his brother Trevor to
bowl the last ball underground"
*Richard Kaufmann*

"Kapil Dev joins Ian Botham in the record books
as the only cricketer to reach the double of 3000
Test runs and 300 Test wickets"
*Richard Keys*

"Whenever I am out of form, I get to play against
India and I regain my form"
*Younis Khan*

"That's the second time Maher has been bitten
— beaten"
*Rod Kilner*

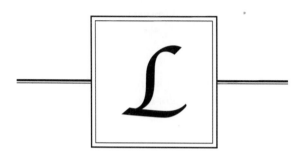

# *Stumped!*

"It's a unique occasion, really — a repeat of
Melbourne 1977"
*Jim Laker*

"An interesting morning, full of interest"
*Jim Laker*

"It's a truism to say that there's been a change in
the weather here at Trent Bridge this morning"
*Jim Laker*

"I was surprised that Geoff Howarth
won the toss"
*Jim Laker*

"I condone anyone who tampers with the ball"
*Allan Lamb*

"I have bowled a trillion overs. I feel like
I am running on fumes at the moment. The
petrol's gone"
*Brett Lee*

"Look, as far as I'm concerned Tendulkar is God,
and if you want to become a better player you've
got to compete with the best"
*Brett Lee*

"Jon Lewis, a real Essex boy there... born in
Isleworth, Middlesex"
*Tony Lewis*

"Kapil Dev seems to have a preconceived idea in his head, but he doesn't seem to know what it is"
*Tony Lewis*

"For any budding cricketers listening, do you have any superstitious routines before an innings, like putting one pad on first and then the other one?"
*Tony Lewis*

"It was all so easy for Walsh. All he had to do was drop an arm and there it was, on the ground"
*Tony Lewis*

"Geoffrey is the only fellow I've met who fell in love with himself at a young age and has remained faithful ever since"
*Dennis Lillee (joking) about Geoff Boycott*

"You can't get any earlier than the second
ball of the game"
*David Lloyd*

"He's a very dangerous bowler — innocuous, if
you like"
*David Lloyd*

"We've had the main course and now it's time
for the hors d'oeuvres and cheese"
*David Lloyd*

"An emotional moment, a marvellous match, a
terrific innings — what can one say on this
historic day?"
*Martin Lock*

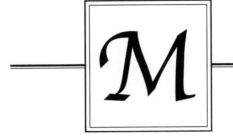

"With the retirement of Dickie Bird something sad will have gone out of English cricket"
*John Major*

"My main problem is Peter. When a fish dies it's the head that starts rotting"
*Bruce Makovah ousted as Zimbabwe's chief selector, with a dig at board boss Peter Chingoka*

"England might now be the favourites to draw this match"
*Vic Marks*

### Christopher Dennis Alexander
### Martin-Jenkins (b.1945)

Sometimes referred to as "Jenkers", Martin-Jenkins is a cricket journalist and commentator for Test Match Special on BBC Radio 4, having joined the team in 1973, aged 28. When he was 17 and captain of cricket at his school (Marlborough) Martin-Jenkins wrote to Brian Johnston asking him how to become a cricket commentator.

"All England want now is a wicket, first and
foremost, and then five more"
*Christopher Martin-Jenkins*

# The world's funniest cricket quotes

"His back injury is behind him"
*Christopher Martin-Jenkins*

"And Marshall throws his head to his hands"
*Christopher Martin-Jenkins*

"It is now possible they can get the impossible
score they first thought possible"
*Christopher Martin-Jenkins*

"At the end of this match at the Sydney ground
the lights have gone out like a flash"
*Christopher Martin-Jenkins*

"And you can't ignore what's going on under the
water of the iceberg either"
*Christopher Martin-Jenkins*

"There was certainly, definitely a suspicion of it
[reverse swing] there"
*Christopher Martin-Jenkins*

"It's his second finger — technically his third"
*Christopher Martin-Jenkins*

"He's got two short legs breathing
down his neck"
*Christopher Martin-Jenkins*

"... where you put a penny in the slot and it gives you an Elvis Presley single like the machines do these days"
*Christopher Martin-Jenkins*
*commentating in 2005*

"If you go in with two fast bowlers and one breaks down, you're left two short"
*Bob Massie*

"Chappell just stood on his feet and smashed it to the boundary"
*Jim Maxwell*

"It was only a brief shower, well, it was briefer than that"
*Jim Maxwell*

"Lillee bowled seven overs, no maidens, no wickets for 35, and I think that's a true reflection of his figures too"
*Alan McGilvray*

"This game will be over any time from now"
*Alan McGilvray*

"It's amazing — when you actually watch a ball you can actually see it a lot better"
*Glenn McGrath*

"I've seen batting all over the world. And in other countries too"
*Keith Miller*

"If there were 22 Trevor Baileys playing in a match, who would ever go and watch it?"
*Arthur Morris*

"Well, everyone is enjoying this except Vic Marks, and I think he's enjoying himself"
*Don Mosey*

"Boycott, somewhat a creature of habit, likes exactly the sort of food he himself prefers"
*Don Mosey*

"He'll certainly want to start by getting off the mark"
*Don Mosey*

# Stumped!

"Dean Headley has left the field with a back
injury... more news on that as soon as it breaks"
*Pat Murphy*

"And he's got the guts to score runs when the
crunch is down"
*John Murray*

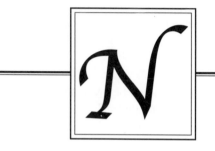

"I might be a shit cricketer, but I'm a shit cricketer in a premiership team, which is more than any of you blokes can say"
*Dave Nadel in the 1981 C-Grade Grand Final*

"Every umpire should be given a computer or a laptop"
*Chandrababu Naidu, India's Chief Minister*

" ... one of the girls has been fingered by officials"
*New Zealand presenter*

"Michael Vaughan has a long history in the game ahead of him"
*Mark Nicholas*

"It's now 2–0 to England with two to play — and they're both to come"
*Mark Nicholas*

"It's a funny kind of month, October. For the really keen cricket fan, it's when you realize that your wife left you in May"
*Dennis Norden*

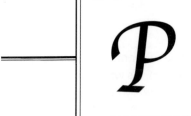

"Cricket is the easiest sport in the world to take over. Nobody bothered to pay the players what they were worth"
*Kerry Packer*

"He's big and raw-boned and I suspect he has the IQ of an empty swimming pool"
*Adam Parore about Andre Nel*

"Sorry, skipper, a leopard can't change his stripes"
*Lenny Pascoe apologizing for bowling bouncers*

"Groins, I'm told, are notoriously bad for never going away. It's something I've had for a couple of years. It disappears for months on end and reappears out of nowhere"
*Min Patel*

### Kevin Pietersen MBE (b.1980)

Pietersen is a cricketer, an attacking right-handed batsman and occasional off-spin bowler who plays for England and Hampshire. He is widely portrayed in the media as having a self-assured personality, and Geoff Boycott once described him as being "cocky and confident". He is noted for his unusual haircuts, with his peroxide-blond streak of hair along the middle of his head being described as a "skunk" (or sometimes even "dead skunk") look.

≈

"I love success. I don't wake up in the morning thinking, 'Great — I've got one million pounds in the bank!'"
*Kevin Pietersen*

"It's a catch-21 situation"
*Kevin Pietersen*

"I don't want to be the next Viv Richards, I just want to be Kevin Pietersen, the best Kevin Pietersen can be"
*Kevin Pietersen*

"A can of Red Bull before I go out to bat, for example, and I am away. What can I say? Life could not be better"
*Kevin Pietersen*

"I found Graeme Smith's attitude pretty childish.
He's a bloke who needs the game but he hasn't
got many friends in it. I don't talk to Smith now.
It's a waste of breath because I don't have any
respect for him"
*Kevin Pietersen*

"It's only a matter of time before the end
of this innings"
*Michael Peschardt*

"Gary never had a nickname — he was always
called either Gary or The King"
*Pat Pocock*

"And as so often with the Achilles tendon
injuries, the Achilles goes"
*Pat Pocock*

"It was close for Zaheer, Lawson threw his hands
in the air and Marsh threw his head in the air"
*Jack Potter*

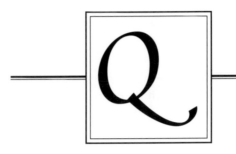

"And there's the George Headly Stand, named
after George Headly"
*Trevor Quirk during a Test between West Indies
and South Africa at Bridgetown*

"Alan Kourie looks calm, but inside his chest
beats a heart"
*Trevor Quirk*

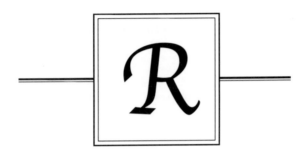

## The world's funniest cricket quotes

"Jack Russell may be the artist, but Metson
showed he's a rhyming couplet of a
wicketkeeper"
*Radio Five Live reporter*

"McCullum dispatched the bails to all four
corners of the hemisphere"
*Radio Sport New Zealand*

"There is, of course, a world of
difference between cricket and the movie
business... I suppose doing a love scene with
Racquel Welch roughly corresponds to scoring a
century before lunch"
*Oliver Reed*

"Border was facing a four-paced prong attack"
*Dave Renneberg for ABC Radio*

"It's a very good witch in Bombay... good wicket"
*Greg Ritchie*

"I played cricket for my local village. It was 40 overs per side, and the team that had the most runs won. It was that sort of football"
*Bobby Robson*

"I'm very concerned for our middle order. We've already called on the immediate next people down, so who do you go to next? I've got a four-year-old son who might like a go"
*New Zealand captain Ken Rutherford after a big defeat by Australia in 1993*

# S

"I am not very aggressive. I play a more boring
kind of cricket"
*Kumar Sangakkara*

"This ground is surprising — it holds about
60,000 but when there are around 30,000 in
you get the feeling that it is half empty"
*Ravi Shastri*

"His feet were a long way away from his body"
*Ravi Shastri*

"A brain scan revealed that Andrew Caddick is
not suffering from stress fracture of the shin"
*Jo Sheldon*

# The world's funniest cricket quotes

"If one-day cricket was pyjama cricket, then
Twenty20 is underwear cricket"
*Navjot Sidhu*

"With his lovely soft hands he just tossed it off"
*Bobby Simpson after Neil Fairbrother hit a single
during a Durham v Lancashire match*

"It's a difficult catch to take, especially when
you're running away from the ball"
*Sky Sports commentator*

"Morning Geraint, how are you?"
*Sky News reporter to Paul Collingwood*

### Kris Srikkanth (b.1959)

Srikkanth made his one-day international debut against England in Ahmedabad in 1981, followed two days later by his Test debut against England at Mumbai. He was a stylish opening batsman with a keen eye and quick reflexes, allowing him to play aggressive attacking strokes with power and precision.

After retirement, he took up the mantle of coaching the India 'A' team. Now he is a broadcaster and a commentator with a sports channel.

≈

"The Zimbabwe-England tie is very important
from India's point of view because, irrespective of
the outcome there, India have to beat England"
*Kris Srikkanth*

"As a captain not in a good form, Sourav Ganguly
should realize that he should play well"
*Kris Srikkanth*

"If Srinath can bowl a little extra pace, it will
make the ball come to the bat more faster"
*Kris Srikkanth*

"Eddie Murphy"
*Kris Srikkanth referring to Brian Murphy*

"Ricky Martin"
*Kris Srikkanth referring to Ricky Ponting*

"Peter Kirsten"
*Kris Srikkanth referring to Kevin Pietersen*

"England players traditionally have been playing
very traditional cricket"
*Kris Srikkanth*

"England players have a typical
English-like attitude, which is different than
Pakistani attitude"
*Kris Srikkanth*

"One needs to understand that test
cricket is test cricket and one-day cricket
is one-day cricket"
*Kris Srikkanth*

"Bradman spent his latter years in Adelaide,
sometimes watching his Australian
contemporaries in action"
*Sky News*

"That one has gone literally through
Michael Clarke"
*Michael Slater*

"England have played pretty well — just their
cricket let them down"
*Ian Smith*

"Chris Lewis didn't bowl, then came in and
scored 30. A top all-round effort"
*Alec Stewart*

"Being on 99 has the habit of turning
sane men into idiots. I said, 'Sorry mate' and
told him I was an idiot"
*Andrew Strauss on his poor call which resulted in
Ian Bell's run out*

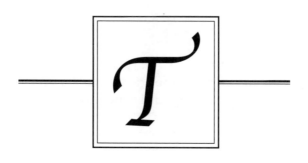

"It was a good tour to break my teeth in"
*Bernard Thomas*

"I knocked his helmet straight off his head. It went to pieces and blood came out... I thought it was brains coming out. I think he was pretty happy to be alive"
*Jeff Thomson*

"The only change England would propose might be to replace Derek Pringle, who remains troubled by no balls"
*The Times*

"With regard to the broken finger, when batting I'll just have to play it by ear"
*Marcus Trescothick*

### Frederick Sewards Trueman OBE (1931-2006)

A Yorkshire and England cricketer, Trueman was regarded as one of the greatest fast bowlers in history. He was the first man to take 300 Test wickets. Known as "Fiery Fred", Trueman occasionally taunted batsmen with his Yorkshire humour and the icy glare that went with his aggressive nature.

Trueman became a popular and rather outspoken radio commentator. Famous for his dislike of many aspects of the modern game, especially one-day cricket, Trueman was criticized by some, such as Ian Botham, for being unduly negative about modern players and for making too much of cricket "in my day".

Trueman was an expert commentator for the BBC's Test Match Special, and his catchphrase "I don't know what's going off out there," summed up his dismay that modern cricketers lacked his knowledge of tactics.

He was made an OBE in 1989. After Brian Johnston, a colleague on TMS, had bestowed on him the nickname "Sir Frederick", there were those who thought he had really been knighted.

"I'm not one to blame anyone, but it was
definitely Viv Richards's fault"
*Fred Trueman*

"That was a tremendous six, the ball was still in
the air as it went over the boundary"
*Fred Trueman*

"People started calling me 'Fiery' because
'Fiery' rhymes with Fred just like 'Typhoon'
rhymes with 'Tyson'"
*Fred Trueman*

"That's what cricket is all about. Two batsmen
pitting their wits against one another"
*Fred Trueman*

# The world's funniest cricket quotes

"Joel Garner, he pockets them for breakfast"
*Fred Trueman*

"The game's a little bit wide open again"
*Fred Trueman*

"We didn't have metaphors in our day. We didn't
beat about the bush"
*Fred Trueman*

"Unless somebody can pull a miracle out of the
fire, Somerset are cruising into the semi-final"
*Fred Trueman*

"If there is a game that attracts
the half-baked theorists more than cricket,
I have yet to hear of it"
*Fred Trueman*

"Anyone foolish enough to predict the outcome
of this match is a fool"
*Fred Trueman*

"Unless something happens that we can't
predict, I don't think a lot will happen"
*Fred Trueman*

"If Boycott played cricket the way he talked,
he would have had people queuing up to get
into the ground instead of queuing up
to leave"
*Fred Trueman*

# The world's funniest cricket quotes

"You can't smoke 20 a day and bowl fast"
*Phil Tufnell*

"Hey Phil, could you lend us your brain? We're trying to build an idiot"
*Heckler in crowd to Phil Tufnell on an England Ashes tour of Australia*

"There were no heroes out there.
They were all heroes"
*Chris Turner talking of the first time he bowled to New Zealand's Martin Crowe*

"The crowd is flocking into the ground slowly"
*Frank Tyson*

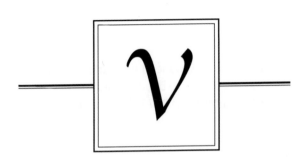

"If I were Freddie, I would try to get a few
of the Aussies out drinking with him because it
will put them off their games. None of the
Aussies could live with him"
*Michael Vaughan with a tip for Andrew Flintoff*

"This achievement we have achieved
is a great achievement"
*Michael Vaughan on beating the West Indies*

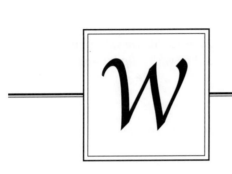

"It is important for Pakistan to take wickets if
they are going to make big inroads into this
Australian batting line-up"
*Max Walker*

"One day there will be radio with pictures"
*Max Walker*

"He has got perfect control over the ball right up
to the minute he lets it go"
*Peter Walker*

"Hardie was a solid rock upon which
Essex hung their caps"
*Peter Walker*

"Peter Booth, who stands to break a personal
milestone in this match ..."
*Peter Walker*

"Binge drinking and teenage pregnancies are the
only games the English invented where they are
still ranked No.1 in the world, and like some of
the dregs who shouted 'cheat' at Pakistan
skipper Inzamam-ul-Haq, some of us would be
better off teetotal"
*Mike Walters*

"Never enough! Whatever it is in life,
it's never enough"
*Shane Warne*

"I didn't drop my pants and moon the crowd; I just went a little bit over the top. I carried on like a pork chop, but the bottom line was I didn't do anything wrong"
*Shane Warne*

"And we have just heard, although it is not the latest score from Bournemouth, that Hampshire have beaten Nottinghamshire by nine wickets"
*Peter West*

"Cricket is basically baseball on valium"
*Robin Williams*

"Australia must now climb to the top diving board for a last desperate throw of the dice"
*Bob Willis*

"This is really a fairy book start"
*Bob Willis*

"The people I had played cricket with, like Paul Allott and Ian Botham, are very keen on pop music of the 1970s. I'd barely heard of, er, who are they... Led Zeppelin"
*Bob Willis*

"Vengsarkar taking a simple catch at square leg, the ball literally dropping down his throat"
*Bob Willis on his balcony celebrations after the win at Trent Bridge in 1997*

"If England lose, they'll be the losers"
*Bob Willis*

"That's what happens when, in cricketing
parlance, the wheel comes off — and you can't
steer the boat"
*Bob Willis*

"He's taking the bull by the horns here, and
throwing everything at it"
*Bob Willis*

On 'The Weakest Link': "When someone
makes a century in cricket how many runs do
they score?"
Contestant: "Two"

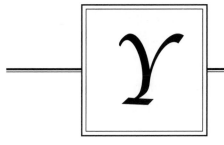

"Hogg suggested we survey the back of the Adelaide Oval, and I don't think he had a tennis match on his mind"
*Graham Yallop on a difference of opinion with his team-mate Rodney Hogg in 1979*

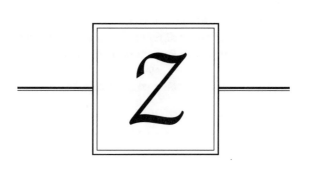

"Anyone who believes President Robert Mugabe will lose sleep over New Zealand not coming to Zimbabwe might as well believe he is not his son's mother or her mother's daughter"
*Editorial in the Zimbabwe Independent*

www.crombiejardine.com

# The World's Funniest Proverbs

JAMES ALEXANDER

Beauty is in the eye of the beer holder

Don't take life too seriously - it's not permanent

Multi-tasking: the art of screwing up everything all at once

Never marry for money; you will borrow cheaper

ISBN 978-1-906051-07-5, £5.99, hb

# The World's Funniest Laws

JAMES ALEXANDER

In Arizona you can go to prison for 25 years for cutting down a cactus!

Do not say "oh boy" in Jonesborough, Georgia. It's illegal!

On Sundays in Florida, widows must not go parachuting!

It is against the law to take a lion to the cinema in Baltimore!

ISBN 978-1-905102-10-5, £4.99, pb